MW00934826

HAPPY
Easter

This Book Belongs To

HAPPY

Easter

ALL PAGES CAN BE COLORED IN FOR EXTRA

FUN!!

I Spy with my little eye something beginning with

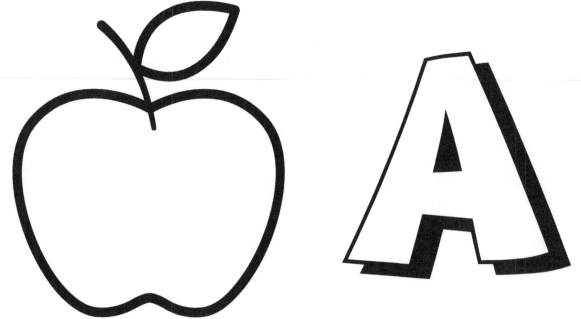

IS FOR

Apple

I Spy with my little eye something beginning with

B

IS FOR

Basket

I Spy with my little eye something beginning with

C

IS FOR

Candle

I Spy with my little eye something beginning with

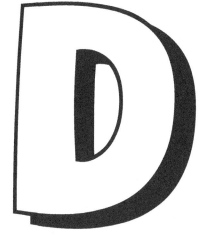

D

IS FOR

Daffodils

I Spy with my little eye something beginning with

IS FOR

Eggs

I Spy with my little eye
something beginning with

IS FOR

Flower

I Spy with my little eye something beginning with

G

IS FOR

Grass

I Spy with my little eye something beginning with

H

IS FOR

Hot Cross Buns

I Spy with my little eye something beginning with

IS FOR

Ice Cream

I Spy with my little eye something beginning with

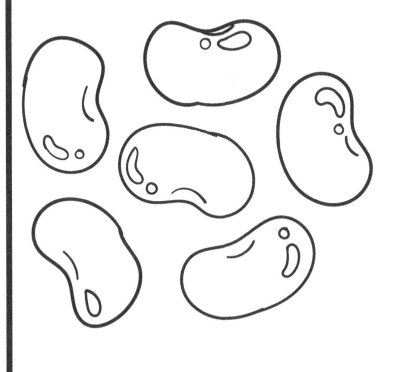

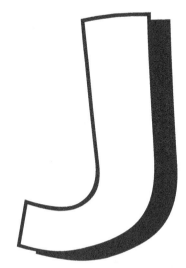

IS FOR

Jellybeans

I Spy with my little eye something beginning with

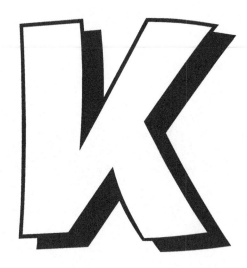

IS FOR

Kale

I Spy with my little eye something beginning with

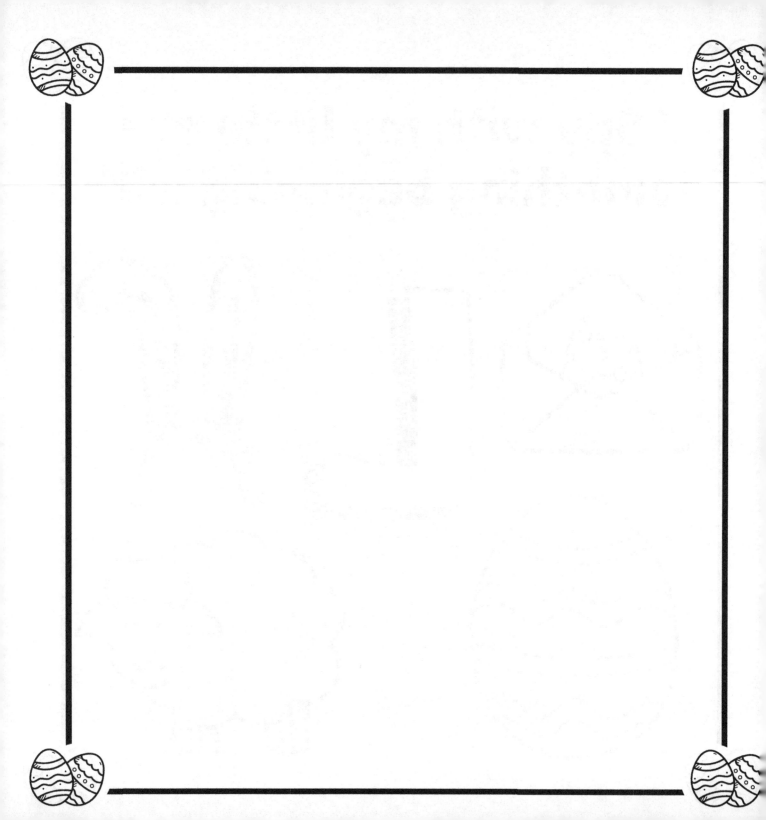

L

IS FOR

Lamb

I Spy with my little eye something beginning with

M

IS FOR

Marshmallow

I Spy with my little eye something beginning with

N

IS FOR

Nesting dolls

I Spy with my little eye something beginning with

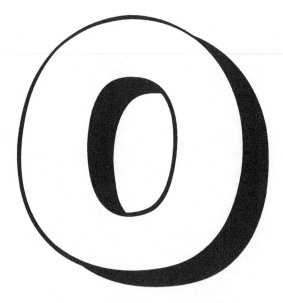

IS FOR

Ornaments

I Spy with my little eye something beginning with

P

IS FOR

Primrose

I Spy with my little eye something beginning with

IS FOR

Quiche

I Spy with my little eye something beginning with

IS FOR

Rabbit

I Spy with my little eye something beginning with

S

IS FOR

Spring Chicks

I Spy with my little eye something beginning with

T

IS FOR

Tree

I Spy with my little eye something beginning with

IS FOR

Umbrella

I Spy with my little eye something beginning with

V

IS FOR

Vehicle

I Spy with my little eye something beginning with

W

IS FOR

Wreaths

I Spy with my little eye something beginning with

X

IS FOR

Xylophone

I Spy with my little eye something beginning with

Y

IS FOR

Yoyo

I Spy with my little eye something beginning with

Z

IS FOR

Zebra

Made in the USA
Las Vegas, NV
22 March 2024